COLLINS LIVING HISTORY

THE ROMAN EMPIRE

Christopher Culpin
Series editor: Christopher Culpin

CollinsEducational
An imprint of HarperCollinsPublishers

Contents

UNIT 1 Winning an empire | page 4

UNIT 2 Living in towns | 14

UNIT 3 Life at home | 26

UNIT 4 Who ran the Empire? | 36

UNIT 5 Rome and the Empire | 46

Glossary | 62

Index | 63

attainment target 1

Questions aimed at this attainment target find out how much you know and understand about the past. Some questions are about how things were different in history: not only people's food, or clothes but their beliefs too. Others are about how things change through history, sometimes quickly, sometimes slowly, sometimes a little, sometimes a lot. Other questions ask you to explain why things were different in the past, and why changes took place.

attainment target 2

This attainment target is about understanding what people say about the past. Historians, as well as lots of other people, try to describe what the past was like. Sometimes they say different things. This attainment target is about understanding these differences and why they occur.

attainment target 3

This attainment target is about historical sources and how we use them to find out about the past. Some questions are about the historical evidence we can get from sources. Others ask you about how valuable this evidence might be.

Introduction

The picture below is a mosaic of two children with a chariot pulled by geese. What does it tell us, as a source, about the Romans? It tells us that they were skilled in making pictures in mosaic, or small coloured tiles. It also tells us what kind of clothes they wore. But does it tell us that they had chariots pulled by geese? Maybe they did, or perhaps this is just a nice picture. Certainly it shows us that the Romans cared enough about children to have things specially designed for them.

This book is about the Roman Empire: the way the people of Rome built up a huge territory. You will also find out about the Romans at home, their food and families. We can find out about this past by using historical sources. In the case of the Romans, we have a wide range of sources and you will find examples of many different types of these sources in this book. You do not have to agree with everything written in this book: you can look back over the pages, especially the sources, and see if you agree.

Winning an empire

The invasion of Britain

In AD 43 the Roman EMPEROR Claudius assembled a large Roman army on the north coast of France. There were 20,000 LEGIONARIES, like the soldier in Source 1, and 20,000 other soldiers, called AUXILIARIES. They were going to invade Britain and make it part of the Roman EMPIRE.

Who would they be fighting against?

The people who lived in Britain at that time were called Celts. They took warfare and fighting very seriously. A Celtic warrior was armed with a spear and a sword, a helmet and a shield, often beautifully decorated (see Source 2).

AIMS

In this unit we will find out about the Roman army and why it was so successful. We will also find out how the Roman Empire grew from the single city of Rome.

SOURCE 1
A modern reconstruction of a Roman legionary ready for battle.

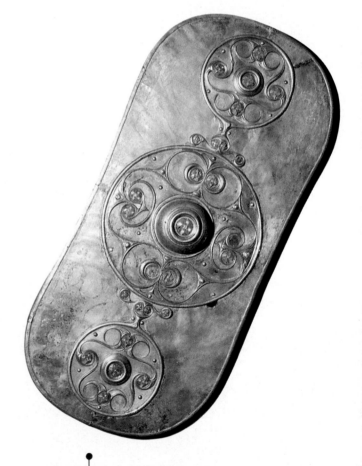

SOURCE 2
A Celtic shield, found in the River Thames near Battersea.

Celtic warriors

A special feature of Celtic warfare was the use of CHARIOTS (see Sources 3 and 4). The chariots could take warriors to any part of a battle, where they would get down and fight on foot.

Celtic warriors were expected to be colourful, dashing and brave. They were always fighting among themselves and different tribes had built their own hill-forts. These were large hill-tops protected by one, two or three lines of steep RAMPARTS, such as the one in Source 5.

'They begin by driving all over the field hurling spears and generally the terror inspired by the horses and the noise of the wheels is sufficient to throw their opponents' ranks into disorder. ...'

By daily training and practice they become so skilled that even on a steep incline they can control the horses at full gallop and stop them in a moment. They run along the chariot-pole, stand on the yoke and get back into the chariot as quick as lightning.'

SOURCE 3

The Roman general Julius Caesar led two Roman expeditions to Britain in 55 and 54 BC. Here he describes Celtic chariot-borne warriors.

SOURCE 4

A modern drawing of a Celtic chariot and warrior. The horses' manes and tails are braided. The warrior is naked and tattooed and holds a shield.

SOURCE 5

An aerial view of Maiden Castle, Dorset. It is the largest hill-fort in Britain.

1 How can you tell from Sources 2, 3, 4 and 5 that the Celts took warfare seriously?

2 How do you think the artist has been able to make the drawing in Source 4?

3 Who do you think would win in a battle between the soldier in Source 1 and the warrior in Source 4?

Roman soldiers

Only a free Roman citizen could become a legionary. Source 6 describes how the army chose recruits. A new recruit joined up for 25 years, during which time he was not allowed to marry. When he retired he would be given enough land to become an independent farmer. He would also have saved some money, although he had to pay for several things out of his legionary's pay.

Look again at the legionary in Source 1. He has half-armour, a shield, a helmet, and tough sandals. His javelin (*pilum*) was thrown at the enemy from a distance and was designed to snap, or bend, on impact. Then it could not be thrown back. His main weapon was a short sword, such as the one shown in Source 9. Source 7 describes how it was used.

In addition to fighting, every legionary had another specialist skill: bridge-building, surgery, book-keeping, wagon-building, arrow-making, ARTILLERY, cooking, arrow-repair, standard-bearer, etc.

> They are taught not to cut with their swords but to thrust. The Romans find it so easy to beat people who use their swords to cut rather than to thrust that they laugh in their faces. For a cutting stroke, even made with full force, rarely kills. On the other hand a stab, even 5 centimetres deep, is usually fatal. Besides, if you attempt to cut with your sword you expose your right arm and side. Yet when you deliver a thrust the body is protected by the shield.

SOURCE 7
This is a description by Vegetius of how Romans used their swords.

> *Gross pay: 248 drachmas (the currency used in Egypt)*
> *Deductions: Bedding   10 drachmas*
> *Food   80 drachmas*
> *Boots   12 drachmas*
> *Annual dinner   20 drachmas*
> *Burial club   —*
> *Clothes   60 drachmas*

SOURCE 8
The pay account for Quintus Julius Proclus Damascenus, a Roman soldier in Egypt, covering four months in AD 81.

> Experts have shown that choosing men is just like choosing horses and dogs. ... The recruit should be broad-chested, with powerful shoulders and brawny arms. His fingers should be long. He should not be pot-bellied or fat-bottomed. His calves and feet should not be flabby. When you find all these qualities in a recruit you can afford to take him even if he is a little on the short side. ... The whole well-being of the Roman state depends on the kinds of recruits you choose.

SOURCE 6
This is a description by the Roman writer Vegetius of how to choose recruits.

SOURCE 9
A Roman sword and scabbard.

Look at Source 8. How much money was Quintus left with (his net pay)?

Legionaries and auxiliaries

Legionaries made up about half the Roman army. The rest were auxiliaries. Auxiliaries were not Roman citizens but came from the provinces of the Empire. They became Roman citizens when they had completed their service. They often had a special local skill in fighting, as archers, SLINGERS, or as CAVALRY, like Rufus Sita (see Source 10). Auxiliaries were usually more lightly armed than legionaries. They had a larger sword, a round or oval shield, and less armour.

SOURCE 11
Tombstone of Marcus Favonius Facilis, a centurion of the 20th Legion, stationed at Colchester. Centurions were tough soldiers, promoted from the ranks. They were responsible for discipline. They were well-paid and moved around the Empire a good deal.

SOURCE 10
The tombstone from Gloucester of Rufus Sita, an auxiliary cavalryman from Thrace (Greece). He was 40 years old and had served 22 years.

The army

There were about 30 legions in the Roman army. Each legion had about 5,000 men, made up as follows:

8 soldiers = 1 *contubernium*

10 *contubernia* = 1 century, commanded by a centurion (see Source 11)

6 centuries = 1 cohort, commanded by a young senator

10 cohorts = 1 legion, commanded by a senator with a second-in-command called an optio.

In addition, each legion had a standard bearer. He carried the gold or silver eagle, the badge of the legion and wore a bearskin. He also looked after the soldier's savings.

The army in action

The best descriptions of the training and discipline of the Roman army (see Sources 12 and 14) come from a Jewish writer, Josephus, who fought against them in the first century AD.

The soldiers were kept fit. Every legionary had to do three 30-kilometre marches a month, carrying 27 kg of kit. Their discipline and training allowed them to carry out special techniques, like the 'tortoise' shown in Source 13.

---

1 What does Josephus say in Source 12 is the most important reason for the Roman army's success?

2 What can you tell from Source 12 about the soldiers the Romans faced?

3 In what ways do Sources 13, 14 and 15 support the statements Josephus makes about the army in Source 12?

' If we look at the way the Romans organise their army it soon becomes clear that this great Empire of theirs came to them as a reward for their great skill, not as a gift of fortune.

The Romans do not sit about waiting for war to break out and then start training men to fight. It is quite the opposite. It is as if they had been born with weapons in their hands. They never stop training and they do not wait for an emergency to arise. What is more, their exercises carried out in peacetime are just as hard-fought as the real thing. Every soldier puts all he has into the training, just as if he were taking part in a real war. That is why their battle formation always holds together; they are never paralysed with fear or worn out with exhaustion.

Their enemies are never a match for the Romans and the Romans inevitably win. In fact it would be true to say that their exercises are bloodless battles and their battles are bloody exercises!

The Romans never expose themselves to surprise attack. Whatever enemy country they may invade, they do not become involved in any battle before they have fortified the camp.'

SOURCE 12
Part of Josephus' description of the Roman army in the first century AD.

SOURCE 13
The soldiers on the left are in tortoise formation. This was used when they were being shot at by an enemy.

Building camps

The marching-camps described at the end of Source 12 can be found all over the Empire. Each soldier dug part of a rampart, and the 'playing-card' shape is always the same, as in Source 15.

'When they are ready to move camp the trumpet sounds and everyone jumps to it. Immediately, at this signal, they take down their tents. A second trumpet call tells them to prepare to march. … The herald asks the troops if they are ready for war. Three times they shout out loudly and enthusiastically 'Yes, we are ready.' Then, in a kind of warlike frenzy they raise their right arms in the air and give a shout. Then they march forward in silence and in good order, with each man keeping his place in the ranks as if they were face to face with the enemy.'

SOURCE 14

Another part of Josephus' description of the Roman army's training.

SOURCE 15

Crop marks showing part of a Roman camp, Great Casterton, Leicestershire. When seen from the air, crop marks show areas that long ago were walls or ditches now destroyed or filled in.

The Roman conquest of Britain

Work in pairs.
The six headings down the left-hand side are all important in a battle. Give the Celts a mark out of 5 for each of them. Then do the same for the Romans. Add up your totals: which side looks most likely to win?
    Discuss your marks with the rest of the class.

	Celts	Romans
Bravery		
Weapons		
Size of army		
Training		
Morale		
Skill of soldiers		
Total		

The crossing of the River Medway, AD 43

The Roman army led by their general, Aulus Plautius, landed unopposed somewhere in Kent. The Celtic leaders, Caratacus and Togodumnus, gathered together as many Celts as they could. We do not know how many. They decided to stop the Romans crossing the River Medway. The river is wide, and in those days there was no bridge.

The Celts were not expecting the Romans to cross the river easily, so were rather carelessly camped on the west bank. The Romans had some auxiliary cavalry from the area we now call Holland. They were used to fighting in watery places. They swam across and attacked the Celts. While the Celts were busy, the Second Legion crossed the river upstream and made a bridge of boats like the one shown in Source 16.

The next day at dawn, more Romans crossed. There was furious fighting and the hero of the Roman attack was Hosidius Geta, an officer. He was nearly captured, but attacked the Celts so fiercely that they turned and retreated to the Thames. Hosidius Geta was rewarded for his bravery.

SOURCE 16
Roman soldiers crossing a bridge of boats.

Taking the hill-forts, AD 43

After crossing the Medway, the Second Legion under their general, Vespasian, moved into the West Country. Here there were many hill-forts, with wide ramparts designed to keep off Celtic warriors using SLINGS.

The Romans used their artillery: the *catapulta* and the *ballista*. The *catapulta* (see Source 17) fired large iron-tipped arrows about 250 metres with great accuracy. The width of the ramparts at Maiden Castle is 150 metres. The *ballista* fired large stones.

The hill-forts therefore presented very little problem to the Romans who rapidly picked them off, one by one.

SOURCE 17
Modern reconstruction of a *catapulta*.

SOURCE 18
Iron tip of a *catapulta* arrow, embedded in the spine of a Celt, found at Maiden Castle, southern England.

The battle of Mons Graupius, AD 84

The conquest of the rest of Britain was not so easy. The tribes in Wales, Northern England and Scotland resisted for a long time. Eventually a new general, Agricola, drove back all opposition. The last battle was fought at Mons Graupius, in Aberdeenshire.

Agricola had two legions, with auxiliary cavalry and infantry, rather fewer in number than the Celts. He led his own men on foot. At first, slings and lances were used, then hand-to-hand fighting. The auxiliary cavalry drove off the Celtic chariots. The weight of Celts began to press the Romans back, so Agricola brought up four more cohorts of cavalry. They broke up the Celts who were defeated.

The Roman writer Tacitus, who was also Agricola's son-in-law, claimed that 10,000 Celts were killed and 360 Romans.

attainment target 1

1 Look again at your marks in answer to the question on page 10. Do you need to change them after looking at the three examples?

2 Can you think of any other reasons why the Romans won?

3 Take any one of the reasons and explain clearly how it helped the Romans to win battles against the Celts.

4 Which reason do you think was the most important for the Romans' success in battle?

5 Some factors are important in a battle (short-term factors); some are important in a long war (long-term factors). Which of the factors here was most important in a battle, and which most important in a war? Explain your choice.

SOURCE 19
A statue of Romulus and Remus with the she-wolf.

The Roman Empire grows

There were 40 PROVINCES in the Roman Empire at its peak (see Source 24). The conquest of Britain, examined in detail in this unit, brought just one more province into the Empire. Sources 20 to 24 show how the Roman Empire grew over the centuries.

The Romans believed that there were two twins, Romulus and Remus, who were abandoned by their parents and raised by a she-wolf (see Source 19). When they grew up, Romulus founded the city of Rome in 753 BC. As Romulus started building the walls of the city, Remus laughed at him and jumped over them. Romulus killed him.

Rome was not independent until about 510 BC when the Romans drove out their powerful Etruscan neighbours. Slowly and gradually, Rome expanded its control over most of Italy. The Romans' expansion into Southern Italy brought them into conflict with the great empire of Carthage.

Three wars were fought between Rome and Carthage over a period of a hundred years. During the second war the Carthaginian leader Hannibal invaded Italy with an army that included elephants. By 146 BC Carthage was defeated and its lands had become Roman provinces. By 133 BC the Romans had also taken over Greece and part of Asia Minor (present-day Turkey).

Rome

Carthage

Roman possessions and colonies

Empire of Carthage

0   500 km

SOURCE 20
Land under Roman control by 264 BC.

SPAIN (Hispanica)   Rome   MACEDONIA

ITALY   ASIA

AFRICA

Roman possessions and colonies

0   500 km

SOURCE 21
Land under Roman control by 133 BC.

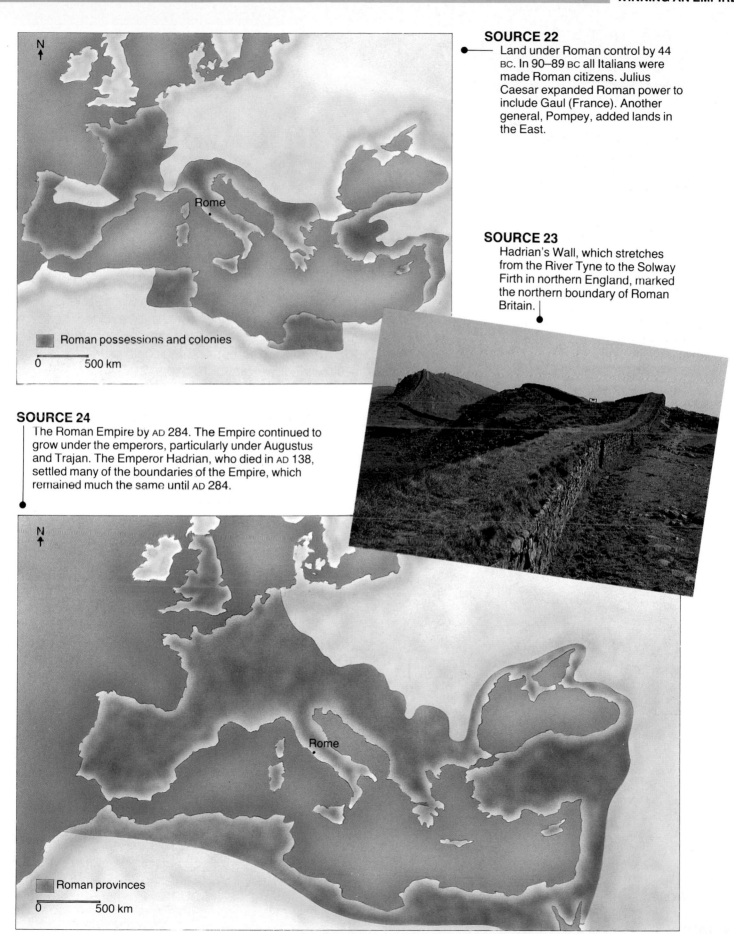

SOURCE 22

Land under Roman control by 44 BC. In 90–89 BC all Italians were made Roman citizens. Julius Caesar expanded Roman power to include Gaul (France). Another general, Pompey, added lands in the East.

Rome

Roman possessions and colonies

0   500 km

SOURCE 23

Hadrian's Wall, which stretches from the River Tyne to the Solway Firth in northern England, marked the northern boundary of Roman Britain.

SOURCE 24

The Roman Empire by AD 284. The Empire continued to grow under the emperors, particularly under Augustus and Trajan. The Emperor Hadrian, who died in AD 138, settled many of the boundaries of the Empire, which remained much the same until AD 284.

Rome

Roman provinces

0   500 km

Living in towns

Pompeii

In the first century AD, on the coast of Italy, south of Rome, there was a prosperous town called Pompeii (see Source 1). It was a peaceful but busy place, having been under Roman control since before 300 BC. The population was about 20,000, making it one of the larger towns in the Roman Empire.

24 August, AD 79 was a holiday in Pompeii. There were athletic events in the morning and plays planned for the afternoon. The town was in an earthquake area. There had been tremors four days earlier and a severe earthquake in AD 62, but nothing could prepare the people of Pompeii for what was about to happen.

AIMS

About 2,000 people died in Pompeii, and those who escaped lost all their homes and possessions. A layer of ash, 6 metres thick, buried the town for the next 1,700 years. But the disaster for the people of Pompeii proved a wonderful source of EVIDENCE **for** ARCHAEOLOGISTS **and historians. The town, now mostly cleared of volcanic ash, tells us a great deal about Roman town life.**

In this unit we will find out about life in Roman towns using evidence from Pompeii and elsewhere. We will also find out why the evidence from Pompeii is so important.

SOURCE 2
Portrait of a man and woman from Pompeii.

SOURCE 1
The Forum at Pompeii, with Mount Vesuvius in the distance.

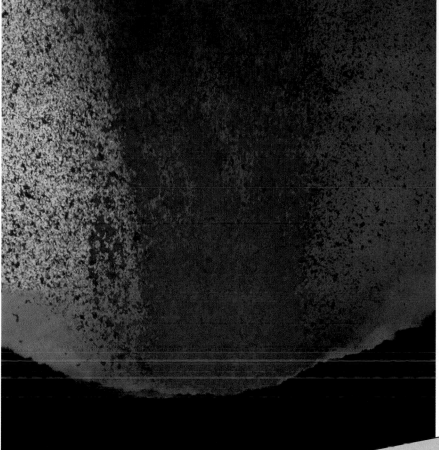

SOURCE 3

A volcano erupting. Mount Etna in Sicily throwing out molten rock and stones.

The disaster strikes

At about midday, when most people were having their lunch, there was a huge explosion. Mount Vesuvius, a volcano which had been quiet for hundreds of years, was erupting. There were bursts of fire and a great cloud of smoke which blotted out the bright sunlight. Soon small stones began to fall on the town, then larger rocks, causing fires and the first casualties. The main cause of death was the hot volcanic ash, which fell in a thick, unending cloud. Most of those who died were choked by the ash and the poisonous fumes which made it impossible to breathe.

Source 4 describes how some people further away felt. At Pompeii it must have been much worse. In the gladiator barracks 34 people died in one room and 18 more in the room where the armour was stored. Two prisoners chained in the punishment cell died there. In the house of Vesonius, the dog, which was chained up with a leather collar, tried desperately to get away, and throttled. The baker, Modestus, had just put 81

'You could hear the shrieks of the women, the wailing of infants and the shouting of men; some were calling their parents, others their children or their wives, trying to recognise them by their voices. People bewailed their own fate or that of their relatives, and there were some who prayed for death in their terror of dying. Many called on the gods for help.'

SOURCE 4

The Roman writer Pliny, then aged 17, was in a town across the bay. He described what the eruption was like.

loaves in his oven to bake; it was to be 1,700 years before they were seen again. Seven children gathered in the house of another baker, Paquius Proculus. They were all killed when the house collapsed. In the biggest house in Pompeii the lady owner collected her jewellery and a silver mirror before rushing outside, only to die in the street with her three maids.

SOURCE 5
A typical street scene in Pompeii today (the houses have been partly rebuilt).

Roman towns

Towns were very important to the Romans. The Roman Empire started from the town of Rome and took over other towns in Italy as it grew. When the Empire expanded into areas where there were no towns, such as Britain, the Romans built towns as a way of spreading their way of life. The word 'civilisation' is based on the Roman word for a town: 'civitas'.

'Two and a half miles further on is Paropeus, if you can call it a town, with no state buildings, no training-ground, no theatre and no market place, where there is no running water and where they live in hovels like mountain huts.'

SOURCE 6
A description by the Roman writer Pausanius of a town in Greece in AD 160.

SOURCE 7
A plan of Pompeii.

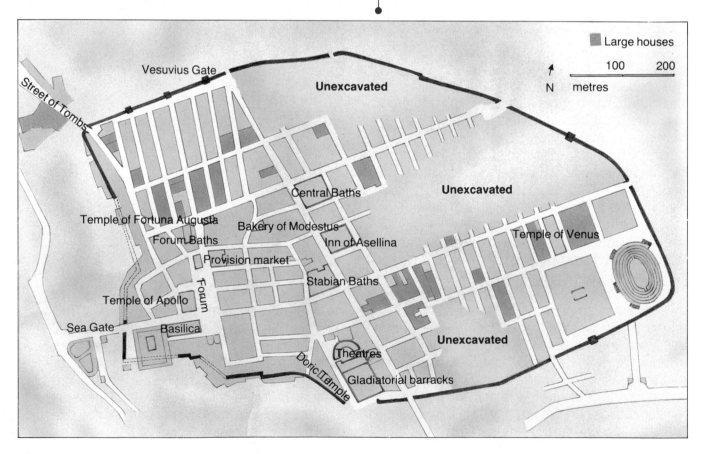

Large houses

100   200

N   metres

Vesuvius Gate

Street of Tombs

Unexcavated

Unexcavated

Central Baths

Temple of Fortuna Augusta

Bakery of Modestus

Temple of Venus

Forum Baths

Inn of Asellina

Provision market

Forum

Stabian Baths

Temple of Apollo

Sea Gate   Basilica

Unexcavated

Theatres

Doric Temple

Gladiatorial barracks

SOURCE 8
An aerial view of the Roman town of Venta Icenorum, near Norwich, England.

SOURCE 9
Plaster-cast of a beggar, found by one of the gates of Pompeii. The dead bodies decayed and left hollow spaces in the ash. Archaeologists pour liquid plaster into the hole, let it harden, then dig away the ash, giving an exact replica of a human being at the moment of death.

SOURCE 10
Walnuts, a loaf of bread and some grain preserved by the volcanic ash that covered Pompeii and found by archaeologists. Cloth, eggshells, needles and shoes have also been found, changed but intact.

' Vibius Restitutus slept here alone and missed his dear Urbana.
Celadus the Thracian [a gladiator] is the girls' heart-throb.
Beware of the dog.
Everyone writes on walls except me.'

SOURCE 11
Graffiti. Just as nowadays people use spray paint to write on walls, so the people of Pompeii scratched and wrote messages on the walls.

> **attainment target 3**
>
> 1 Use Source 6 to explain what facilities the Romans expected a Roman town to have.
>
> 2 Use Sources 5 and 7 to describe what the streets of Pompeii were like.
>
> 3 Compare Sources 5 and 7 with Source 6. How far does Pompeii seem to live up to Pausanius' ideas of what a town should be like?
>
> 4 What types of historical sources do archaeologists have from Pompeii?
>
> 5 Which of them would not be found at the site of the Roman town at Venta Icenorum (Source 8)?
>
> 6 What can historians find out about the Romans from Pompeii which they are unlikely to find out about in any other way?
>
> 7 Write a list of reasons why the site at Pompeii is a very useful site for historians of Roman towns.
>
> 8 Why is it important for historians to look at evidence from other towns, apart from Pompeii, as well?

Forum and basilica

Look again at Source 1, and find the forum and the basilica on the plan of Pompeii in Source 7. The forum was the market and meeting place of the town. It was open in the middle, with a covered walk supported by columns at the sides. Here were shops and offices (see Source 14).

The basilica was always next to the forum. It was a large hall, with a grand entrance (see Source 12). Here the town council met, and law-courts were held. There were also offices for the government of the town.

As we will see in unit 3, only rich Romans lived in their own large houses. Most townspeople lived in small, inconvenient flats or rooms. This meant that they spent as little time there as possible, living most of their lives in the streets and forum.

The warm Mediterranean climate also made this a pleasant way of life.

It was usual for rich townspeople to spend their own money on making the town more beautiful and better equipped. For example, Marcus Ulpius Carminus, of Aphrodisia, gave 150,000 denari to improve his town. The money was spent on new fittings for the basilica, cleaning and improving the forum, and on new seats for the theatre.

Fine public buildings were another reason for spending time about the town, and not in your own home.

Romans got up early, so soon after dawn the forum would be busy with people: shoppers, peasants coming in from surrounding villages, buskers and street performers, rich men and women with their personal slaves, and ordinary Pompeiians just meeting for a chat.

SOURCE 13
Decoration from public buildings, Bet Shean, Israel.

SOURCE 14
A reconstruction of the forum and basilica at Caerwent, South Wales.

Shops

SOURCE 15

A row of shops in Pompeii, only partly excavated. You can see the street was paved, with a raised pavement on each side. There are stepping stones for pedestrians to cross the street.

SOURCE 16

A Roman carving of a butcher's shop. The butcher is serving an important customer. The scales, for weighing meat, are hanging up, as are the various joints.

SOURCE 17

The market halls at Lepcis Magna, North Africa.

SOURCE 18

A snack-bar. Containers of food were put in the holes and could be kept warm. Cooking facilities in people's flats were not good, so many Romans bought a snack – a slice of pork, some bread and olives, or cheese – at a street snack-bar.

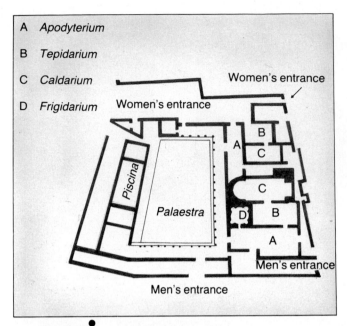

A *Apodyterium*

B *Tepidarium*

C *Caldarium*

D *Frigidarium*

SOURCE 19
Plan of one of the baths at Pompeii.

Baths

To a Roman, an important part of civilised life was the baths. Here people could meet, relax and chat as well as getting clean. Pompeii had several public baths, like the one in Sources 19 and 20.

The visitor would go straight to the changing room (*apodyterium*). After that he or she could exercise in the exercise yard (*palaestra*), or go straight into the baths. First came the cold bath (*frigidarium*) then the warm room (*tepidarium*). Then there was the hot bath (*caldarium*). The water was heated in a boiler over a furnace which also heated the rooms. The bather could then sit and sweat, before rubbing oil on. This was then scraped off, with all the dirt, using a *strigil* (see Source 21).

SOURCE 20
Caldarium in the baths at Pompeii.

SOURCE 21
Oil pot and strigils.

'My lodgings are right over the bath house. Imagine all the noises, loud enough to make me hate my ears. I can hear the grunts of the men exercising by lifting lead weights ... or the slapping of hands on bodies when someone is having a massage. ... Then you've got the man who loves to hear his own voice in the bath, or the chap who plunges into the pool with an enormous splash, as well as the shrill voice of the manicurist advertising his trade. ... The only time he stops his chatter is when he's plucking armpits – and then it's the customer who's screaming.'

SOURCE 22
The baths were a popular place for meeting friends and relaxing. The Roman writer Seneca gives this description.

Water supply

The Romans knew that fresh water was important, not only for bathing but for drinking. There were drinking fountains on many street corners in Pompeii. There were public lavatories, too. Some were only a large jar fastened to the wall, which was emptied regularly. Others were flushed with running water, like those in Source 23.

The city of Rome was served by eleven AQUEDUCTS, bringing water down to the city from springs in the hills. One, the Aqua Marcia, supplied 1¼ million litres an hour. All over the Empire aqueducts like the one in Source 24 were built to bring water into the towns the Romans founded. The water had to flow gently down to the town, and the Romans were expert water engineers. They built bridges to carry the water over river valleys and could use SYPHONS and air-locks.

SOURCE 23
A marble-seated public lavatory.

SOURCE 24
Remains of an aqueduct at Oudnagare, Tunisia.

Sport and entertainment

We can see from Source 7 that Pompeii had two theatres and an AMPHITHEATRE. In the open-air theatre (see Source 25) canvas covers kept the sun off the audience. Perfume was often sprinkled on the seats to overcome the smell of sweat. Plays sometimes included music and the scenery was mounted on the high wall at the back of the stage. Theatres were large, and the actors wore masks. This helped members of the audience sitting far away from the stage to see the characters clearly (see Source 26). However, the design, based on Greek theatres, meant that everybody in the audience could hear every word.

1 Why do you think smaller, covered theatres were more common in Britain?

2 What characters do you think the actors in Source 26 are playing?

SOURCE 25
Model of the ruins of Pompeii showing the large open theatre (left) and covered theatre (right).

SOURCE 26
A scene from a comedy. The actors are wearing masks, and there is a flute player in the centre.

SOURCE 27
The amphitheatre at Pompeii.

SOURCE 28
Advertisement, found on a wall in Pompeii.

20 pairs of gladiators will fight in combat
The property of Lucretius Satrius Valens
Plus
10 pairs of gladiators
The property of Lucretius, son of Valens
Plus
Full-scale animal hunts

Gladiators

The most common type of entertainment offered in the amphitheatre (see Source 27) was a fight, usually to the death, between two gladiators. Gladiators were slaves, or prisoners captured in war, or condemned criminals. Rich Romans would pay for a number of gladiators to be kept and trained to fight (see Source 28). The most common fight was between a heavily-armed gladiator and one with only a net, trident and dagger, as in Source 29.

The gladiators paraded at the beginning of the show and saluted the most important person at the show with the words 'Hail! We who are about to die salute you'. The fighting then began.

Amphitheatres were also used for shows involving mock battles, hunting and fights with wild animals. Some of the most spectacular shows were in Rome and you can read about them in unit 4. These shows were very popular, but some Romans protested (see Source 30).

SOURCE 29
Mosaic of gladiators. The defeated gladiator would raise his finger, asking for mercy. If he had fought well the crowd gave the 'thumbs pressed' sign, and he was spared. If they gave the 'thumbs twirled' sign, he was killed. A gladiator who had won many fights could be given a wooden sword. If he was a slave he was freed, if he was a free man he could retire.

Once I happened to go to the Midday Games hoping to see something different from the usual bloodshed. It was the exact opposite ... this was pure murder, and in deadly earnest. When one man falls another takes his place, and this goes on and on until none are left. You may say that one committed a robbery ... that one committed murder. Even so, does he deserve to die like this? What sort of punishment do you deserve, you wretch, for watching him?

SOURCE 30
An attack on gladiatorial shows by the Roman writer Seneca.

SOURCE 31
Mars, god of war.

SOURCE 32
Juno, queen of the gods.

Temples and religion

The early Romans believed in many different spirits and gods. In unit 3 we will find out about the spirits of each home and family. As their Empire grew the Romans came across other religions and often took over their beliefs. The twelve gods and goddesses of the Greeks were combined with the Roman gods and given Roman names:

Jupiter, king of the gods
Juno, queen of the gods
Neptune, god of the sea
Minerva, goddess of science and craft
Mars, god of war
Diana, goddess of the moon and hunting
Apollo, god of the sun and prophesy
Venus, goddess of love
Vulcan, god of metal-working
Vesta, goddess of fire
Mercury, god of communication
Ceres, goddess of agriculture

Priests and sacrifices

Temples like the one in Source 33 did not hold large numbers of worshippers, but were places where the PRIESTS carried out religious ceremonies. The priests were not a separate group of people: they were rich and important people in the town or city who paid money for the honour of serving in the temple.

On special days devoted to the god or goddess, people would go in a procession to the temple, like the one shown in Source 34. The priests would sacrifice animals. They would then examine the internal organs of the dead animal and 'read' messages from the god or goddess in what they saw.

SOURCE 33
Temple of Jupiter, Rome.

SOURCE 34
A carving of a religious procession.

SOURCE 35

A model reconstruction of a small villa near Pompeii. The Roman word 'villa' means a farm. This farm near Pompeii specialised in producing wine: you can see the huge jars in the courtyard on the right. There is a house for the family and their workers or slaves, and other farm buildings.

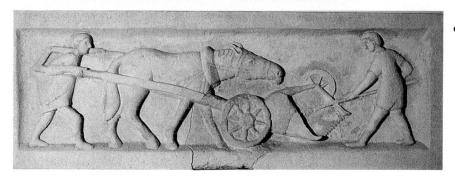

SOURCE 36

This carving from a Roman area of Germany seems to show a kind of horse-powered harvesting machine. There are written descriptions of such a machine, but no remains of it or other carvings have been found anywhere else.

Out of town

Farms in the countryside, like the one in Source 35, produced the food for those living in the towns. Some Roman landowners owned huge estates, covering thousands of acres. Caius Calcilius Isidorus, a freedman who died in 88 BC, owned 3,600 pairs of oxen, 257,000 other animals, 4,116 slaves and 60 million SESTERCES in cash. The Roman general Ahenobarbus offered 10 hectares of land to each of his soldiers from his own estates. There were at least 4,000 soldiers in his army.

At the other extreme were poor PEASANTS struggling to survive on 6 or 7 acres. Somewhere in between came a farmer like Ausonius, who owned land near Bordeaux in France. He had 50 hectares of corn, 24 hectares of vines, a meadow and 160 hectares of woodland.

Farming

Most farm-work was done by hand, as it was through all the centuries of history until recently. Land was ploughed with a simple ox-drawn plough. Crops were harvested with a scythe or sickle. There were books in Roman times to pass on good ideas for farming (see Source 37).

SOURCE 37

Advice for farmers from the Roman writer Columella.

'Lean land which is level and well-watered should be ploughed first before the end of August then gone over a second time in September and made ready for sowing about 21 September.

Double-rowed barley is sown in the richest possible areas, but in cool areas not until the month of March.'

Life at home

Food and cooking

The Romans were very sociable people: they enjoyed meeting their friends and relaxing together. As we have seen, they met socially in the streets and the forum, and in the baths. As the Roman writer Martial shows in the letter to his friend Julius Cerealis (see Source 1), they also met socially in their own homes. They enjoyed food of all kinds, as the people living by the Mediterranean do nowadays (see Source 3).

Source 2 is a reconstruction of a kitchen in a big Roman house. The stove is on the right, with an oven and a griddle, a bit like a barbecue. Flour was kept in the large jar on the left, wine, oil and other liquids in the *amphorae* (the long jars with pointed ends to left and right). One of these would contain *liquamen*, a kind of fishy sauce the Romans added to many of their dishes.

AIMS

In this unit we will find out about the Romans as people, their homes and personal lives. We will find out particularly about what families were like, and how the men, women and children in families related to each other.

We will also look at different kinds of sources and learn how to deal with pieces of evidence that seem to say different things.

SOURCE 2
A modern reconstruction of a Roman kitchen.

SOURCE 1
A letter by the Roman writer Martial.

' To Julius Cerealis,
You'll get a good meal, Julius, at my place; so if you've nothing better to do, come. Keep the *eighth hour* free; we'll go to Stephanus' baths beforehand, just next door. For first course you'll get lettuce, fresh young leeks, salted tunny fish, a little bigger than a mackerel and garnished with eggs and parsley; more eggs, this time baked to a turn with Velabran smoked cheese and Picenum olives ... So much for starters. Do you want to hear the rest? Well, if I tell a lie or two perhaps you'll come. For the main course there'll be fish and oysters, chicken, duck – things that our friend Stella only serves for special meals. And I promise not to read you any poetry after dinner.'

eighth hour: about 2 p.m.

SOURCE 3
A market stall near Naples in Italy today.

Daily meals

Breakfast was simply a roll, lunch only a mid-morning snack, such as bread and cheese, or something from a street snack-bar. For the main meal poorer people ate soups and stews as a way of making small and cheap ingredients go further. A typical meal for better-off Romans is described in Source 1.

There was a great variety of types of food available locally as well as rare delicacies from all over the Empire. In Rome, for example, there was even a huge range of types of bread: honey bread, oil bread, suet bread, cheese bread, large grainy Cilician loaves, soft, salty yeast bread, mushroom-shaped loaves and poppy-seed loaves, pancakes, split rolls, wafers with wine, pepper and milk and square loaves with aniseed, cheese and oil.

Romans ate in the *triclinium* (see page 34), half-lying down, on couches. They ate with one hand, not with a fork or spoon. This meant that sauces had to be thick, not too runny, and dishes often included pastry or bread to act as a scoop. Wine was the usual drink.

SOURCE 4
Roman glass bowl and bottle.

'A tray was brought in with a whole wild pig on it, with two little baskets hanging from its tusks, one full of dry dates, the other of fresh dates. A bearded servant then drew a hunting knife and pierced its side, whereupon a number of thrushes flew out.'

SOURCE 5
A description of one of the courses at a banquet given by Trimalchio, an enormously rich man in a story by Petronius.

Banquets

Very rich Romans would show off with enormous and exotic banquets, like the one described in Source 5. Sometimes guests who had eaten too much would go into another room, vomit, and then eat more.

Clothes and hair

The toga (see Source 6) was worn only by men of the upper ORDERS (see unit 4). It was a single piece of material 6 metres long and 1 ½ metres wide. You needed a servant to help you put it on, it was difficult to wear and only seen on formal occasions. Underneath the toga, and around the house, men wore a simple tunic reaching just above the knees. Working men wore simple, tough clothes. As you can see from the pictures of Roman men in this book, most were clean-shaven with short hair.

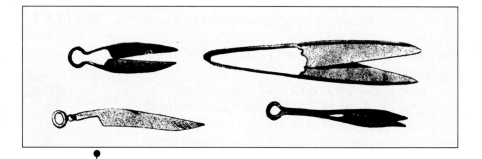

SOURCE 6
A statue of a Roman man of the upper orders, wearing a toga.

SOURCE 7
Barbers' shears and razor.

SOURCE 9
Many Roman women had elaborate hairstyles.

How do Roman hairstyles, for men and women, differ from hairstyles of people today?

SOURCE 8
A carving of a Roman woman of the upper orders, wearing a stola. The stola was a long woollen garment, reaching to the feet, worn with a belt. Underneath it women wore a bra and girdle.

The family and the law

Men had a dominant role in Roman society, and particularly in the family. The head of the family, always a man, was the *paterfamilias* (see Source 10). He had power over his wife and other relatives, however old they were, as well as the house slaves. In law, none of his household could do anything important without his consent.

The *paterfamilias* usually arranged the marriages of sons and daughters. When a woman married, her father paid a DOWRY, usually a small amount of money, to the husband. She left the control of her father and came under the control of her husband and his *paterfamilias*. She could not own anything in her own right. Men, too, had no right to own property while their father was alive.

This picture of men and women in families is based on what Roman law said (see Source 11). In practice things were not quite like that.

SOURCE 10

The *paterfamilias*. In this sculpture the *paterfamilias* carries portraits of his ANCESTORS. This was to remind him and his family to live up to the standards and achievements of previous generations.

What do members of your class think about the old Roman law in Source 11?

'The old law made married women do exactly as their husbands wished and made husbands rule their wives as if they were possessions. If a wife was good and obeyed her husband in everything she was as much mistress of the house as he was master. … But if she did anything wrong, the man she had wronged was her judge and decided what punishment she would receive.'

SOURCE 11

Part of the old Roman law on men and women.

> attainment target 2

Modern archaeologists and historians have produced a rather different picture of Roman family life.

A Archaeologists looked at hundreds of tombstones and INSCRIPTIONS. They found:
- **Men's tombs:** names of wives are rarely found on the tombs of men who died in their 20s. Wives' names are much more common on the tombs of men who died in their 30s and older.
- **Women's tombs:** names of husbands are found on the tombs of women who died in their teens, 20s and older.

B Historians have run computer simulations using the following facts: LIFE EXPECTANCY was 36 for men, 28 for women. A quarter of all babies died before reaching the age of one. Women could legally marry at 12, men at 14. They found:
- One in three children had lost their father by the age of 10.
- One in 20 children had lost both parents by the age of 10.
- Four in five men had lost their fathers by the time they married.
- Half the women had lost their fathers by the time they married.

1 What does the evidence in A tell us about the age men and women got married? How do you think this would affect relations between husbands and wives?

2 What does the computer simulation in B suggest about the power of fathers? What does it suggest about sons' and daughters' rights to do what they wanted?

3 How does this picture of Roman family life differ from that described on this page? Give reasons for the difference.

4 Which do you think is more accurate? Explain your answer.

Women

The large difference in life expectancy between men and women was probably due to the dangers of childbirth. Most women in Roman times would have been pregnant, or recovering from childbirth, for all their married lives. Many mothers died in childbirth. Even if the mother survived, the death of babies and children must have been distressing for them. For example, of 164 inscriptions on tombs in the Jewish cemetery in Rome, 65 are of children under 10. Even the emperors were affected: Marcus Aurelius had five sons, four of whom died as children.

Many richer couples seem to have practised some kind of birth control, perhaps because of the dangers of childbirth.

SOURCE 12
This writing tablet is from the wife of the commanding officer of Vindolanda to her friends at home.

Life for the rich

Richer women could have an easy life, if they wished. They had to run the home, which meant telling the household SLAVES what to do. Even looking after the children was handed over to female slaves. If her husband moved around the Empire because of his job, she would go with him. Source 12 is a writing tablet from such a wife at Vindolanda, a fort on Hadrian's Wall in Britain.

Rich women spent a good deal of time and money on their appearance as the items in Sources 14 and 15 show. This brought some of the same kinds of jokes from men that we hear today (see Source 13).

> You live at home, Galla, but not your beauty – that lives at the chemists. Well, take your hair, that's made far away in Germany. At night you put your teeth away just like your dresses. When you get into bed the rest of you is boxed up in a hundred little boxes – even your face sleeps in a different place.

SOURCE 13
A poem by Martial from 1st century AD.

SOURCE 14
Painting of a girl pouring scent into a bottle.

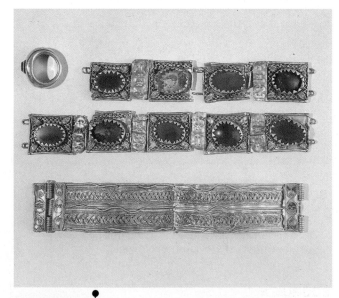

SOURCE 15
Gold bracelets and a ring found at Rhayader, Wales.

What was life really like for women?

As we saw on page 29, half of all women had no father alive when they married. They may well, therefore, have been able to choose their husbands. By the first century AD marriage was less strict and divorce was more common. Women may well have had money of their own and could hold on to it when they married (unlike the situation in Britain before 1882). However, women could not vote, or have any job in government.

It is hard to find out what relations between husbands and wives were really like. We can get some idea from letters and tombstone inscriptions, such as those in Sources 16, 18, 19 and 20, but these, of course, only refer to rich couples.

' Here lies Amymone, wife of Marcus, most good and beautiful, wool spinner, obedient, modest, careful, chaste, a woman who stayed at home.'

SOURCE 16
An inscription from a tomb in Rome.

SOURCE 17
Jet medallion, found at York, showing husband and wife.

I do not doubt that it will be a source of great joy to you to know that Calpurnia has turned out to be worthy of her father, worthy of you, worthy of her grandfather. Her carefulness and good sense is of the highest. She loves me – a sign of her purity; to these virtues is added an interest in literature which she has taken up out of fondness for me. She repeatedly reads and even learns by heart my works.

SOURCE 18
Pliny, who was in his 40s, was married to Calpurnia, who was in her late teens. He wrote this to Calpurnia's aunt, who was his own age.

' I know I don't write to you as often as I should. The reason is that I am so unhappy at present that whenever I write to you or hear from you, I go to pieces completely and can't bear it. ... If the present troubles are going to last then the one thing I want is to see you, my love, as soon as I can...

But what's going to become of my little Tullia? ... And what will Marcus do? How I long to have him in my arms or on my knee. I can't write any more, I am too upset. ... Goodbye, dear Terentia, best and most devoted wife.'

SOURCE 19
Cicero wrote this to his wife, Terentia, his daughter Tullia and son Marcus, in 58 BC. He and Terentia had been married for 20 years.

You must now be father and mother, hide your tears and kiss away the children's. My children, if your father remarries you must try to approve, win over your stepmother by your good behaviour and not praise your own mother. If he does not remarry, then he will soon be old, and try to be cheerful and supportive.

SOURCE 20
Here Propertius imagines an 'ideal' wife and mother, Cornelia, writing to her husband and children after she has died.

1 What does Source 12 tell us about the education of girls from rich families?

2 How reliable are Sources 16 and 17 as evidence of Roman husbands' attitudes to their wives?

3 How would you describe Pliny's attitude to his wife (Source 18)?

4 How would you describe Cicero's attitude to his wife (Source 19)?

5 What else would you need to know about Pliny and Cicero in order to decide on the reliability of Sources 18 and 19?

6 Use Sources 16 to 20 to describe what the ideal Roman wife was supposed to be like.

7 In this unit there are sources of different types: a letter from a woman (Source 12), men's written comments (Sources 13, 18, 19 and 20), a painting (Source 14), a tomb (Source 16) and a medallion (Source 17). All are useful in their way in finding out about Roman women. Explain the usefulness of each source.

Ordinary women's lives

For poorer women life was centred round the continual hard work of children and home. Looking after the fire, cooking, cleaning, washing, spinning, weaving, making clothes and caring for the children were her tasks. Without any modern appliances all these jobs were hard physical labour. They were essential for the family's survival. In that way wives and husbands were partners. However, it was a partnership dominated by the husband.

Children

It is difficult to find out much about the lives of children. A few toys have been found, so some parents were obviously prepared to have things specially made for their children, such as the chariot in Source 21.

In Sources 19 and 20 parents speak about their children with affection. Some people put their children's portraits on their tombs (Source 22).

What do Sources 21 and 22 tell us about parents and children?

SOURCE 21
A model chariot.

SOURCE 22
Tomb of Julia Velva, York.

SOURCE 23

A Roman carving of four scenes from childhood. On the left the baby is fed by the mother, while the father looks on. Later the father cares for him. As a child he learns to drive a little cart pulled by a goat. At about the age of seven he goes to school. Many of the teachers were Greeks.

Families and children

In poorer families children helped around the house as soon as they were able to. When they were older they were then expected to go out to work. Sons were regarded as more important than daughters: they could earn more. Daughters would need to have a dowry provided for them when they married.

For very poor people children could be a liability. Sometimes they sold unwanted children to be slaves, or even killed them.

Rich parents also wanted small families, but for quite different reasons. The normal system of inheritance was to divide property equally between heirs. A large family would mean dividing up property into small lots, which was inconvenient. This may be another reason why rich families practised birth control. Smaller families also meant that more care could be given to each child.

As we have seen, many children had no father by the age of 10 and many had lost both parents. Other members of the family would usually bring them up. Many would have had no father alive when they grew up. This had a good side: instead of a strict old *paterfamilias* running your life, a young man or woman could take his or her own decisions.

SOURCE 24

Tombstone of Laetus' daughter from Bordeaux, France. Notice the girl's pet cockerel at the bottom of the tombstone.

Houses and homes

Most people in towns lived in flats, either in a block of flats like the one in Source 25, or in a flat over a shop (see unit 2, Source 15). The flats were small, inconvenient, without running water and sometimes badly built. There were often fires from the open wood-burning cooking stoves.

A survey of Rome in the fourth century AD listed 47,000 blocks of flats and only 1,800 houses. In a prosperous town like Pompeii there was a bigger proportion of houses (see unit 2, Source 7). Nevertheless, only a minority of Romans lived in a 'typical' Roman house like the one in Source 26.

SOURCE 25
A model reconstruction of a Roman block of flats in Ostia, the port of Rome.

SOURCE 26
A Roman house.

1 Entrance hall
2 The atrium. This was a small courtyard usually open in the middle, with a pool for rainwater. Most rooms opened off it.
3 The *tablinum*. This was usually the grandest room in the house, with mosaics and wall-paintings. Here the owner would receive people on business and do his own work.
4 Bedrooms – usually small, with little furniture.
5 The peristyle. This was a small garden, perhaps with fruit trees, surrounded by a covered walk with columns.
6 The *triclinium*. The dining room, also richly decorated.
7 Kitchen.
8 This space let out as a shop with a separate entrance.

SOURCE 27
Mosaic from the entrance to a house in Pompeii. It says 'beware of the dog'.

SOURCE 28

Shrine of the household spirits (the Lares and Penates). The Lares were the spirits of the family and its ancestors. The Penates protected the food store. It was the job of the *paterfamilias* (see Source 10) to make daily offerings to the Lares and Penates at the shrine. This made sure that the good reputation of the family was kept up and the food store was full.

SOURCE 29

Peristyle from a house in Pompeii.

Who ran the Empire?

Rome

In this unit we will find out what kind of government the Roman Empire had. We will also find out how this changed over the years.

Rome was the centre of the whole Empire, and the Forum (Source 1) was the centre of Rome. The model in Source 2 shows that Rome was not as carefully planned as Pompeii (unit 2). Rome's population grew enormously as the Empire expanded. By the first century AD there were about 1 million people in Rome, and it was by far the biggest city of the Empire. It was a teeming mass of people from many lands, as Seneca complains in Source 3.

SOURCE 1

A view of the Forum at Rome today.

SOURCE 2

Part of a model of how Rome might have looked about AD 300.

Houses, blocks of flats, shops and markets were jumbled up together. Among them, as you can see in Source 2, were grand public buildings, mostly put up by the emperors. On the right you can see the Circus Maximus built for chariot racing, which could hold 250,000 spectators. Just right of centre is the Colosseum, built about AD 80 by the Emperors Vespasian and Titus. It held 50,000 people, watching gladiator fights and other spectacular events.

Because it was the centre of the Empire, Rome was the centre of government. It was events in Rome that decided who should rule the Roman Empire.

> Look at the crowds for whom ... there are hardly enough houses. The majority of them are foreigners. They have flooded in from the country towns of Italy, in fact from all over the world. And their motives for coming? A hope to get on in the world ... a good rich opportunity for vicious living. Some come to Rome for education, others for the games; some to be near their friends, others – workers – because Rome gives them greater scope for displaying their skill. ... Every sort of being has come here ... Most of them, you will find, have left home and come to Rome, the greatest and loveliest city in the world – but not theirs.

SOURCE 3
A description of the people in Rome by the writer Seneca.

SOURCE 4
A poem by Juvenal from the 1st century AD.

> There's nowhere a poor man can get any quiet in Rome. School teachers with their shouting wake you up at dawn. At night it's the bakers, and all day long it's the coppersmiths with their hammers banging. On one side of the street there's the moneychanger idly rattling his coins while on the other side the goldsmith's beating gold plate with his mallet. There's an incessant stream of soldiers, drunk as lords, ship-wrecked sailors wrapped in bandages, beggars and sellers of sulphur with tears pouring down their cheeks.

1 What impression of Rome do you get from the sources on these pages?

2 What complaints about Rome do the authors of Sources 3 and 4 make?

3 How serious do you think they are?

Who was who in Roman society?

Member of Parliament

Mayor

Religious leader

Landowner

Business executive

Crossing patrol person

Bus driver

Teacher

Nurse

Headteacher

If you look at the picture above and answer the questions on this page, you will probably find that your top three important people in each case were not always the same. Why do you think that is? Did anyone come in the top three in more than two groups?

Clearly people can be important for different reasons, or for a mixture of reasons. It was just like this in Roman society. They had strict divisions between the different groups, which they called ORDERS. These orders were based on several things:

- Family history. The order you belonged to depended on the order your parents or even grandparents were in.
- Money. The people at the top were richer.

- Law. Different orders had special rights (see Source 6).
- Behaviour. Romans believed that the higher the order you were in, the better behaved you had to be. This meant being serious, respectable and living a good life.

---

1 Which three of the ten people above are the most important to you?

2 Which three of them are the richest?

3 Which three of them are regarded by adults as the most important?

4 Which three of them have the most power?

Senators

SENATORS had to have at least 1 million SESTERCES, which meant they were rich. They were mostly landowners. For many years all the senators came from the great senatorial families of Rome. In the first century AD men from other parts of Italy and the older Roman provinces were made senators.

Senators wore a toga with a wide purple stripe. They could not marry a woman who was, or who had been, a slave. The top jobs in running the Empire, such as governor of a province, or commander of a legion, were reserved for senators. They could not take part in public performances in sport or on the stage. They had special privileges, such as the one described in Source 6.

SOURCE 5
A statue of Marcus Tullius Cicero, a famous senator.

' The emperor issued special instructions to prevent the disorderly system by which spectators got seats for shows. He was outraged by the insult to a senator, who, on entering the crowded theatre at Puteoli was not offered a seat by a single member of the audience. A new law provided that at every performance the front row of the stalls must be reserved for senators.'

SOURCE 6
An extract from a life of the Emperor Augustus by the Roman writer Suetonius.

1 Look at the points about the orders at the bottom of page 38. Explain how each of them applied to senators.

2 Why was the law described in Source 6 passed?

Knights (*equites* in Latin)

Knights had to have at least 400,000 sesterces in money. They had to have parents or grandparents who were not slaves. Knights wore togas with a narrow purple stripe, and had a gold ring.

Important jobs in the government of the Empire and in the army were reserved for them. Money was not the only thing that mattered. Taking care of their towns was also important and a lot of money was lavished on places of worship and amenities.

Some knights were richer than senators. For example, Marcus Nonius Balbus (see Source 7) was the richest man in Herculaneum, a town near Pompeii. He built the basilica and baths there at his own expense.

SOURCE 7
Statues of Marcus Nonius Balbus, knight, and his mother Vicinia.

A carving of a draper's shop. On the right the two assistants hold up the material. A couple from the upper orders are sitting down to look at it, each with their own slave.

Plebs and liberti

These were the great mass of the rest of the people, doing every job from shopkeepers to farmers, sailors to miners. Plebs and liberti were usually poor. The Roman writer Seneca thought the rich ought to know just how poor, as he explained in Source 9.

Freed slaves

Liberti were freed slaves. It was quite common for masters to free their slaves when they died, or after a number of years' service. Slaves could also buy their freedom. Liberti could not serve in the army, although plebs could. As we have seen, liberti could not move any further up the orders, or marry into a senator's family, although their children could.

Some liberti were quite rich, even very rich. A clever and devoted slave, who had given good service might be set up in business by his or her master. They might do well and become rich, like Trimalchio in the story by Petronius in Source 10.

Some liberti had great power, like Callistus, Narcissus and Pallas, the three secretaries to the Emperor Claudius. But they were still inferior to all except slaves, given the worst seats at celebrations, the worst food at a dinner.

As we have seen, family status was very important to the Romans. These liberti were clever, but many Romans bitterly resented ex-slaves becoming so powerful.

'You should sleep on a poor man's mattress; your cloak should be threadbare and you should try eating the hard, cheap, grimy bread the poor have to eat. Believe me, you'll jump for joy and feel you've had a good meal.'

SOURCE 9
Part of Seneca's advice to the rich about how the poor lived.

I decided to go into the shipping business. I had five ships built and loaded them with wine, which was fetching a high price at that time, and shipped them off to Rome. What a disaster! In one day the old sea god Neptune swallowed down a million's worth of wine. But I wasn't beaten, not me. I built more ships, bigger, better and luckier. … My wife lent me all her money and I shipped a cargo of wine, bacon, beans, perfumes and slaves.

SOURCE 10
Part of the story of Trimalchio by Petronius.

1 Describe the clothing of the different people in Source 8.

2 What does Source 10 tell us about the wealth of Trimalchio, a freed slave, and his wife?

3 Why didn't senators or knights do what Trimalchio did?

Slaves

Slaves were really non-people: they could be bought and sold like goods or animals.

An owner could treat slaves badly, beat them or even kill them. If a slave attacked his or her owner all the slaves in the household were put to death, even if they had nothing to do with it. Slaves could not own anything, or make a will to pass on anything to their family. The worst-treated slaves were in industry, like those described in Source 11.

Household slaves

Slaves could do important jobs: for example, Julius Caesar appointed slaves to run the Mint (which controlled the making of coins). Free people would not do this work as they thought accounting was beneath their dignity. Some household slaves were treated well by more sensitive Romans such as Pliny (see Source 12).

Some historians have suggested that having slaves held back progress in Roman times. Why invent new machines and new ideas if you can get someone to do the work for nothing? Do you think this is true?

SOURCE 13
A tombstone to a slave called Martinus.

Their skins were seared all over with the marks of old floggings, as you could see through the holes in their ragged shirts. ... They had letters marked on their foreheads and half-shaved heads and irons on their legs.

SOURCE 11
A description by the Roman writer Apuleius of slave workers in a flour mill.

'I am very upset by the illness which has carried off some of my slaves recently, some of them only young. I get some comfort from two things: first, I've always been ready to grant my slaves their freedom; second, I let my slaves make out their own wills which I carry out as if they were legal.

I know there are some who look on this misfortune as simply losing money, and still think they are men of wisdom. I don't know about them being wise, but men they certainly are not.'

SOURCE 12
Part of a letter from Pliny about his household slaves.

1 Why did the slaves in Source 11 have marked foreheads and half-shaved heads?

2 What is Pliny's attitude to his slaves?

3 What does he tell us about other people's attitudes to their slaves?

4 What does Source 13 tell us about another Roman's attitude to a slave?

SOURCE 14
Julius Caesar.

Senators and emperors

In the early days of Rome's history the city was ruled by kings, the first of whom was Romulus (see unit 1). In 510 BC the people of Rome rose up and threw out the last king. From then on Rome was ruled by the senators, who met in a council called the Senate. The plebs also had a council, so the badge of Roman government became SPQR (*Senatus Populus Que Romanum*). This means 'The Senate and the Roman people'.

As we saw in unit 1, Rome built up its Empire in a long series of wars. Unfortunately, the success and size of the army led the generals to want to take power for themselves. Between 100 BC and 50 BC there were terrible CIVIL WARS, with Roman killing Roman. The Senate could not stop them.

Julius Caesar

Out of this chaos came someone who put an end to the violence by seizing all power himself: Julius Caesar (see Source 14).

Caesar had made a tremendous success of conquering Gaul (France) for the Empire. The Senate, worried that he would do the same as other generals, forbade him from entering Italy. But in 49 BC he crossed the Rubicon, the river marking the boundary of Italy, and marched to Rome. He took control of the city, defeated his rival Pompey, and was made DICTATOR for life.

ACTIVITY

We have seen that Rome had several types of government. Each had its advantages and disadvantages. For example, rule by the Senate had the *advantage* of giving all the top people some say in running the country; rule by dictator had the *disadvantage* of taking power away from everyone else.

Get into groups of four.

1 Discuss the advantages and disadvantages of each type of government using the table:

2 Are there times when one system of government is better than another, for example, in war, or peace?

	Advantages	Disadvantages
Senate	Top people all have a say	?
Dictator	?	No-one else had any say in the government
Rule by all people (rich and poor)	?	?

The first emperor

Julius Caesar was popular and successful in bringing peace and order. But some senators clung to their old, traditional system. On 15 March (the Romans called this date the Ides of March) 44 BC, Julius Caesar was stabbed to death.

The ASSASSINATION of Julius Caesar brought more civil war, until another strong man emerged to take control. This was Julius Caesar's nephew, Octavian. In 27 BC he became the first emperor, taking the name Augustus.

Augustus' rule

Augustus ruled from 27 BC to AD 14. He clearly set about making his power secure:

- He gave presents and extra money to the army.
- He increased the privileges of senators (see Source 6) and gave them the impression he was consulting them, although in fact he made all important decisions himself.
- He spent money on making Rome beautiful. He said 'I found a city of brick and left it a city of marble.' 82 temples were built or re-built, as well as baths, libraries, aqueducts and markets.
- He encouraged the worship of the emperor as a god and encouraged traditional Roman religion (see Sources 16 and 17).

SOURCE 15
A coin of the assassins. It shows the daggers, the cap of liberty and the date of Caesar's death.

SOURCE 16
A model of the Temple of the Emperor Claudius at Colchester, England.

SOURCE 17
Augustus as priest. Augustus stands left of centre, with his toga drawn over his head, at a religious ceremony. The bull will be sacrificed to the gods in the old way.

- He tried to appear a traditional Roman. He encouraged the family and made it harder to get divorces. He tried to ban excessive luxury and spending on clothes and banquets. Augustus himself led a simple life, wore ordinary clothes and slept on a low, plain bed.

- He used poets and artists to get his ideas across. Many of Rome's greatest poets were writing during his time as emperor. He encouraged Vergil (see unit 5, Source 10) to write his long poem, *The Aeneid*. This tells the heroic story of the origins of Rome. The poet Horace wrote poems about simplicity, purity and the dangers of wealth. Statues of Augustus, like the one in Source 18, showed him as a great, noble and brave man.

- His policy to the ordinary people of Rome has been called 'bread and circuses'. There had been hand-outs of bread to the poor before, but Augustus increased and widened them. 250,000 people were given a hand-out of bread every day. At the same time he organised lavish games and free shows, as he says in Source 19.

'Three times I gave a show of gladiators. On 26 occasions I gave to the people, in the circus, in the forum or in the amphitheatre hunts of African wild beasts in which 3,500 wild beasts were killed. I also gave the people the spectacle of a naval battle on the River Tiber.'

SOURCE 18
The Emperor Augustus.

SOURCE 19
Augustus' listing of his games and free shows for the people of Rome.

SOURCE 20
Mosaic of animals attacking people tied up, and of humans hunting animals.

1 How did Augustus' 'bread and circuses' policy win the support of the people of Rome?

2 Explain why Augustus carried out *each* of the seven policies above.

3 How much did the Empire change between 100 BC and AD 14 (see Unit 1)?

4 How did the government of Rome change in that time?

5 What things did Augustus change when he came to power? What things did he leave alone?

6 Who benefited from the changes he brought?

7 Many of the things Augustus did (building temples, holding games, giving out bread) were not new. Does that mean that he brought no important changes to Rome?

8 What do you think was the most important change which Augustus brought? Explain your answer.

SOURCE 21

Augustus and his successors. Augustus is shown at the top. In the centre, below, is his son Tiberius, emperor from AD 14 to 37. Augustus' greatgrandson, Gaius, known as Caligula, is shown as a child in the bottom left-hand corner.

Who should follow?

One of the problems of one-person rule, by a dictator or an emperor, is what to do when that person dies. Often there are struggles and wars until another leader wins through. One answer to this problem is to hand over power at once to one of the children, usually a son, of the dead emperor. But sons do not always have the abilities of their fathers, and what if the emperor died childless?

These problems dogged Rome for the rest of its existence. Some emperors were bad, for example Gaius, called Caligula (see Source 22).

On the other hand the Emperor Hadrian, who ruled from AD 117 to 138, worked hard for Rome. He travelled widely throughout the Empire, made frontiers more secure and brought a lasting peace (see Source 23).

'As soon as he gained power as emperor, Hadrian immediately took up the policy of the first emperors and devoted his energies to maintaining peace. . . . He came to Britain and put right many things that were wrong. He built a wall 80 miles long, to keep the BARBARIANS and the Romans apart.'

SOURCE 23

An extract from a biography of Hadrian compiled in the 4th century.

SOURCE 22

The Emperor Gaius (Caligula) who ruled between AD 37 and 41. He was cruel and suspicious. He had people arrested and put to death for no reason. He declared himself a god and attacked people who refused to worship him. The imperial bodyguard murdered him in AD 41.

Rome and the Empire

Travel and trade

In unit 1 we saw how Rome built up a large empire. As Source 3 shows, travellers could go from one end of the Empire to the other on good roads. The boats in Source 1 carried goods in large quantities across the seas of the Empire. All this travel and trade was centred on Rome.

By the first century AD, the Romans controlled lands and peoples which were very different from their city in Italy. Strabo, in Source 2, clearly regarded many of these people as savages whom the Romans had civilised.

SOURCE 1
Mosaic of two Roman cargo ships passing a lighthouse.

SOURCE 2
This was written about the Romans by Strabo, who lived in Asia Minor (now Turkey) in the 1st century BC.

'The Romans took over many nations that were naturally savage owing to the places they lived in, because those places were either rocky, or without harbours, or cold. Thus they not only brought into contact with each other peoples who had been isolated, but also taught the more savage how to live under forms of government.'

SOURCE 3
The Peutinger map. There was a large map of the Empire carved in marble in the Forum in Rome. This is part of that map, copied on to parchment. It is more a diagram, like a London Underground map, than an accurate picture. It shows the main rivers and towns and the roads between them.

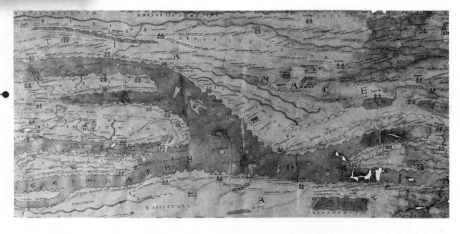

The spread of ideas

The symbol ☧ is made from the first two letters of Christ's name in Greek: XP (= ChR). Christianity is a religion which started in the Middle East. Source 4 is part of a wall-painting found in Kent, in southern England. What does this tell us about the way ideas and beliefs travelled in the Roman Empire?

The Christian belief in only one God meant that Christians could not worship the Roman gods, including the emperor. The Romans were tolerant of some religions, but PERSECUTED Christians. Many were killed, sometimes by wild animals in the arena, but Christianity could not be stamped out, and gained more and more support.

1 Describe the cargo boats in Source 1. How were they powered? How were they steered?

2 What does the lighthouse tell us about trade and travel in Roman times?

3 How do you think the light in the lighthouse was made?

4 In Source 2, Strabo thinks that people living in certain places were savage because of where they lived. What kinds of places? Do you think he is right?

5 What effect, does he say, did the Romans have on them?

6 Try to find and read some of the names of places in Source 3. Compare it with a modern map. There are obvious differences, but are the routes the same?

SOURCE 4
Chi-Rho symbol from a wall-painting from Lullingstone villa, Kent.

Why build an empire?

Nowadays our government's answer to questions like this is put in terms of money: does it make a profit? We have huge government departments to work out the cost of everything the government does. To the Romans, financial profit was only one reason for conquering new lands. Even if the emperor wanted to know if a province was bringing Rome a profit he couldn't find out. He did not have a government department to collect the information.

Adding Britain to the Empire

In 55 BC and 54 BC Julius Caesar came to Britain with some of his army. He was investigating what would be involved in conquering this land and joining it to the Empire. Sources 5 and 7 give some different opinions about whether it would be worth the effort.

In fact, it was to increase his reputation that Claudius eventually launched an invasion in AD 43, 97 years after Julius Caesar's expedition. Finance did not come into it, and Britain probably cost the Romans more than they ever received from the island. There was always at least one legion in Britain, which was expensive. The Emperor Nero seriously thought about pulling out of Britain but dare not lose a province of the Empire, even if it was costing a lot of money.

Other writers found other motives for building up an empire (see Sources 9 and 10). They emphasised the benefits the Romans brought to conquered peoples.

> Grain, cattle, gold, silver and iron are found in the island. They are exported, together with hides, slaves and excellent hunting dogs. ... At present we collect more in from the customs duties on their trade than we could by direct taxation, because this would mean maintaining an army to garrison the island and collect the taxes.

SOURCE 5
Strabo writes about Britain.

SOURCE 6
Roman sculpture of hunting dogs.

> There is no hope for booty other than slaves, among whom you cannot expect any highly skilled in literature, or music.
> Glory in war exceeds all other forms of success; this is the origin of the Roman people's reputation, this is what ensures our city will have eternal fame, this has caused the world to submit to her rule.

SOURCE 7
Cicero thought only about what the Romans could grab from a new province, and was not enthusiastic about Britain.

> The coasts and interiors have been filled with cities. ... As on a holiday, the whole civilised world lays down the weapons which were its ancient burden. ... It is possible for all, with or without property, to travel wherever you wish. Neither inaccessible mountains, nor immense stretches of river, nor tribes of BARBARIANS cause terror ... You have spanned the rivers with all kinds of bridges and cut highways through the mountains. You have accustomed all areas to a settled and orderly way of life.

SOURCE 9
A description of the benefits of the Empire by Aelius Aristides, a Greek who lived in the 2nd century AD.

SOURCE 8
Collecting taxes in Germany.

'Others no doubt will better mould the bronze
To the likeness of soft breathing, cut from marble
A living face ...
or learn to measure
Better than we, the pathways of the heavens,
The rising of the stars. Remember, Roman,
To rule the people under the law, to establish
The way of peace, to battle down the proud,
To spare the humble. Our fine arts, these, forever.'

SOURCE 10
An extract from Vergil's poem, *The Aeneid*.

1 The only writer here to think about the profit or loss involved in conquering Britain was Strabo (Source 5). What did he decide?

2 What did Cicero think of Britain as a source of slaves (Source 7)?

3 List the benefits of Roman rule outlined in Sources 9 and 10.

4 Which of the writers in these sources would have agreed with Claudius about invading Britain in AD 43?

5 What do these sources tell us about the attitudes of Romans towards the Empire and those outside it?

What did Rome get from the Empire?

As we saw in unit 4, Rome was a huge bustling city of 1 million people. It had to be supplied with goods from far and wide, as the map in Source 11 shows.

In unit 4 we saw that the emperors arranged a daily hand-out of flour to 250,000 poor people in Rome. This meant importing an enormous quantity of grain. Egypt alone sent 150,000 tons of grain a year. Large cargo boats had to be built, like those in Source 1. Such a boat could carry up to 400 tons of grain, or 10,000 jars of wine or oil. With good winds it could sail from Egypt to Ostia (the port for Rome) in nine days.

The Greeks were more experienced seafarers than the Romans, and usually operated the ships. At Ostia there were huge warehouses and the grain was sold to dealers.

Water transport was used throughout the Empire because ships could carry bulky items cheaply.

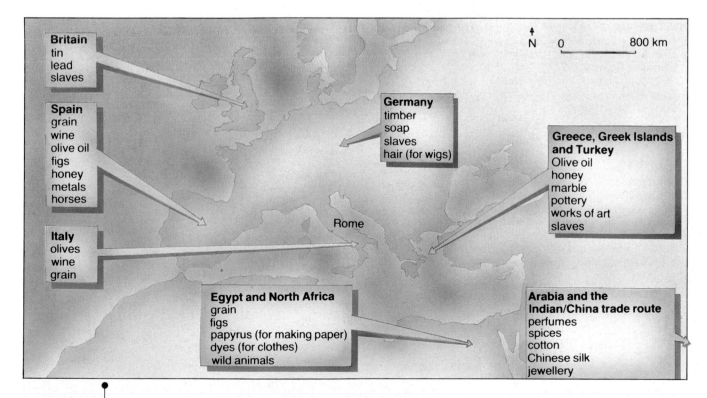

SOURCE 11
Goods supplied to Rome by the provinces of the Empire.

Roads

All over Europe the lines of Roman roads can still be seen, such as the one in Source 12. Roads were usually built by soldiers. Source 14 shows an imaginative reconstruction of road-building.

'Some are busy felling trees and clearing hillsides, others are cutting and stacking stones, while stone masons cement the stones together. Others work hard to divert the course of streams. The countryside is filled with the noise of workmen.'

SOURCE 13

A description of road-building in Italy, written for the Emperor Domitian in AD 80.

SOURCE 12

An aerial view of the line of a Roman road in England. In Britain alone the Romans built 16,000 kilometres of road. They were built as straight as possible to allow the army to march quickly.

SOURCE 14

A modern drawing of soldiers building a road. The route was first surveyed by an *agrimensor*. He made sure the road was straight by using lines of poles. Soldiers would then cut a furrow, and remove trees from each side. This was to avoid an ambush.

The road was built up on an embankment, called an *agger*. The road was then laid, with ditches at each side and a 'camber' or slope on it for drainage. Main roads were 9 metres wide, minor roads about 3.6 metres.

SOURCE 15
Paved surface of a Roman road at Blackstone Edge, Lancashire.

'The ox was the chief traction animal (used for pulling wagons) ... the mule and the donkey were rivals, the horse hardly at all. All three were slow and hungry. ... Figures suggest that a wagon-load of wheat would double in price in 300 miles. Not even the famed Roman roads, built for military, not commercial reasons, made any significant difference since the means of traction remains the same.'

SOURCE 16
Professor Finlay.

---

1 How far do Sources 13 and 14 give us the same information about Roman roads?

2 What details are there in each source which is not in the other one?

3 Do you think the artist of Source 14 had read Source 13?

4 Which do you think is the more reliable description of road-building?

5 How would an historian make use of Sources 12, 13, 14 and 15?

The striking fact about trade and industry in Roman Britain is the ease with which problems of transport were overcome. Wherever manufactured, goods were easily distributed throughout the province. These facts point to the skilled development of carts and wagons ... and to the efficient maintenance of the road system.

SOURCE 17
Professor Frere.

Travelling on roads

Once a province was conquered the military need for roads was less. They were still important for letters between Rome and the Roman governors of the provinces. These were carried in light, fast carts. Inns were set up along all major roads to provide rest for messengers, and a change of horses. Private letters were not carried, except in exceptional circumstances.

Nowadays governments build roads to help trade and industry. As we have seen, these were not the reasons why Romans built good roads. Nevertheless, better roads could have helped trade and industry in Roman times. Historians disagree about this (see Sources 16 to 18).

... oysters. Their shells appear in almost every Roman site. They imply an efficient and fairly rapid use of road transport, for if they were carried in tanks of water they were very heavy; if without water, then they required reasonable speed of delivery before they were dead and dangerous.

SOURCE 18
Professor Salway.

attainment target 2

1 In what ways do Sources 16 and 17 disagree?

2 Which one does Source 18 support?

3 What other evidence would you look for to try to see which view was more correct?

Outside the Empire

Julius Caesar's expeditions of 55 and 54 BC had shown the Celts in Britain how powerful the Roman army was. He had then gone back to France, but for how long? Where did the future lie?

Some in the Hampshire area became friendly with the Romans and traded with them. Source 19, a coin of their leader Verica, shows a Roman-style horse, and the vine leaf, symbol of the Roman wine they loved. Others remained hostile to Rome. Source 20 shows a coin of Cunobelin who ruled a large area of South-East England. It shows a Celtic horse and an ear of barley, used for making beer, which the Romans despised.

Celts in other parts of Britain were out of contact with Rome and had little to do with them. There were the same mixed reactions to the eventual Roman conquest of Britain in AD 43. Some, like Caratacus, fought the Romans with all their might until they were defeated. Others, like Boudicca's family, started by being friendly. Then, realising that their whole religion and way of life was being undermined, they rose in a massive rebellion in AD 60. Boudicca led her followers to sack and burn the Roman towns of Colchester, London and St Albans before she was defeated.

However, some threw in their lot with the Romans from the beginning, and stayed loyal. They could enjoy all the benefits of Roman civilisation.

One of these was Cogidumnus, who probably built the huge palace at Fishbourne (see Source 21). Italian architects, gardeners and mosaic designers made it the most spectacular Roman site in Britain. Source 22 shows one of the palace's black and white mosaics, made in a style then very fashionable in Italy.

SOURCE 20
Coin of Cunobelin.

SOURCE 19
Coin of Verica.

SOURCE 21
A modern model of Cogidumnus' palace at Fishbourne, Sussex.

Romans and race

Romans divided people into three types: those who were outside the Empire were regarded as BARBARIANS, or 'savages' (see Source 2). Then there were 60 million or so people inside the Empire, of whom five or six million were Roman citizens. The citizens were again divided into 'orders' (see unit 4). The Romans were quite arrogant about these divisions. They were convinced their way of life was best. But they did not discriminate against people because of the colour of their skin.

By the first century AD there were many black people inside the Empire, and black Roman citizens. We have no means of knowing the colour of people who left inscriptions, but the altar in Source 23 may well have been put up by a black man from North Africa.

People from Italy, France, Spain, Holland, Yugoslavia, Greece, Turkey, Syria and Algeria (using modern names for these areas) lived in Britain in Roman times. Source 24 shows the tomb of Regina, a Celtic slave-girl bought and freed by Barates, a Roman soldier from Palmyra in Syria.

SOURCE 22
Mosaic from Cogidumnus' palace.

'To the spirit of the place, to the fortune the home-bringer, Eternal Rome and the god of fate. From the province of Mauretania Caesarensis, Caius Cornelius Peregrinus, town councillor.'

SOURCE 23
From an altar found at Maryport, Cumbria.

SOURCE 24
The tombstone of Regina, found in South Shields, Tyneside. Underneath the Latin is a line in Barates' Palmyran lettering.

Romanisation

After Boudicca's revolt was crushed, the Romans set about persuading Celtic warriors and chiefs to live in Roman style. None of them lived in quite the style of Cogidumnus, but many began to enjoy the benefits of Romanisation (see Sources 25, 26 and 30).

The centres of Romanisation were the towns: London, Colchester, St Albans, Silchester, Cirencester, Leicester, Winchester, Wroxeter and Dorchester, among others. The great baths at Bath were also built (see Source 28).

In Source 27 Tacitus includes knowing how to speak Latin as an important part of Romanisation. Private tutors taught Latin to the children of the rich. Young men who joined the army would learn Latin too, but Source 29 provides some evidence that writing Latin went further than this.

> In order to get the Celts to live in peace, enjoying life's pleasures, Agricola encouraged individuals and helped local communities to build temples, market places and houses. He praised hard workers and scolded the lazy. He had the sons of the tribal chiefs educated. ... So it was that a people who at first rejected the Latin language became keen to speak it fluently. In the same way our clothes became popular, and the 'toga' came into fashion. Gradually the British were led astray. What they thought was civilisation was, in fact, making them slaves.

SOURCE 27
The Roman historian Tacitus describes how Agricola, his father-in-law and Governor of Britain, encouraged Romanisation.

SOURCE 28
The Roman baths at Bath.

SOURCE 25
Decorated beaker.

SOURCE 26
Glass vase.

SOURCE 29

A piece of pot with a hole so that it could be worn on a bit of string and with graffiti scratched it. It reads 'Verecunda the actress loves Lucius the gladiator'.

> Mosaics decorated the floor of at least the dining room; warmed by braziers, the householder could entertain his guests to dinner in some degree of fashion. While sampling the products of a more varied diet they could discuss, in Latin, the subject of his new wall-painting.

SOURCE 30

A modern historian, J. Wacher, describes the effects of Romanisation.

However, it would be wrong to think that the Romanisation described in Source 27 affected everyone. Poor farmers, and people in Cornwall, Wales, northern England and Scotland were hardly affected by Roman rule. Source 31 shows an imaginative reconstruction of a farmstead in Northumberland in Roman times.

SOURCE 31

Modern reconstruction of a farm at Riding Wood, Northumberland, in Roman times.

attainment target 2

1 Which aspects of the Roman way of life did the Celts accept?

2 Give one fact and one opinion from Source 27.

3 This author says that it is wrong to think that Romanisation affected everyone. How does this statement give a different view of Roman Britain from Source 30. Suggest reasons for these differences.

4 Which of the two views do each of Sources 25, 26, 28, 29 and 31 support?

SOURCE 32
Three Celtic gods. The three figures wear typical Celtic cloaks. This carving was found at the Roman fort at Housesteads on Hadrian's Wall.

SOURCE 33
The inscription on an altar found near Hadrian's Wall. Sylvanus was a combined Roman and Celtic god of the countryside.

'To the unconquered Sylvanus ... if he were to capture a remarkably fine boar which others have failed to catch, this altar is set up by Gaius Tetius Veturius Micianus, prefect of the Sebosiana Auxiliary Cavalry.'

Rome and Christianity

The story of this unit is one of give and take between Rome and the peoples that they conquered. The same give and take took place in religion. Temples to the Roman gods were set up in the provinces. At the same time Romans joined in worshipping local gods, like those in Sources 32 and 33. Some provincial religions spread across the whole Empire. A temple to the Persian god Mithras, for example, has been found in London.

The rise of Christianity

Only men could become worshippers of Mithras, but Christianity had a wider appeal. After the death of Jesus Christ in AD 33 his followers, especially St Paul, spread his ideas across the Empire.

One of the reasons for the success of Christianity was that anyone could be a Christian. man or woman, master or slave. But the belief in only one God meant that they refused to worship the emperor. This brought savage PERSECUTION at times, as Sources 34 and 35 describe. In Rome the Christians hid in the Catacombs (see Source 36). Elsewhere Christians had to hide or find help where they could (see Source 35).

First, Nero had some Christians arrested. Then, on their information, large numbers of others were condemned. Dressed in wild animals' skins, they were torn to pieces by dogs, or crucified. ... Nero provided his gardens for the spectacle and exhibited displays at the Circus where he mingled with the crowd.

SOURCE 34
The Roman historian Tacitus, writing about the year AD 64.

At the time when the Christians were being persecuted by the emperors, Alban received into his house one of the clergy who was in flight from his persecutors. When Alban saw him devoting himself day and night to prayer he was suddenly touched by the presence of God and began to follow his example of faith and piety ... leaving behind the darkness of idolatry, he became a Christian with all his heart.

SOURCE 35
An extract from Bede's *History of the English Church*, written in the seventh century. Alban was arrested and charged with hiding the priest. He was beheaded outside the town we now know as St Albans.

SOURCE 36
Christ and the apostles, from a wall-painting in the
Catacombs in Rome. These are natural caves underneath
the city. Here Christians hid and worshipped in secret.

The Christian Empire

In the fourth century the Emperor Constantine
became interested in Christianity and allowed
Christians to worship freely. In 335 he made
Christianity the official religion of the Empire.
From then on the Roman Empire was also a
Christian Empire.

Sources 35, 37 and 38 show that Christianity
spread to Britain, too.

SOURCE 37
The head of Christ from a mosaic found in Dorset.

1 Why do you think persecution of the Christians failed
to wipe them out?

2 Why do you think Christianity appealed to the people
of the Roman Empire?

3 What were the advantages to Christians of their
religion becoming the official religion of the Empire?

SOURCE 38
Christian bowl, vase, strainer and plaques from the
Roman town of Water Newton, Cambridgeshire.

The decline of the Empire

In the third century AD the Roman Empire went through a difficult time.

- There were long civil wars between generals who wanted to become emperor.
- It became harder to find men willing to serve in the legions.
- Prices rose: a measure of corn worth eight drachmas in Egypt rose to 120,000 drachmas. The cost of being a senator or a knight became too high. People began to refuse to serve in the government.
- Evidence shows the population seems to have been declining.
- The northern frontiers of the Empire were under serious attack. Tough warlike tribes of Goths, Vandals and Franks raided the Empire with increasing success.
- The eastern frontiers of the Empire came under attack from the Persian Empire under a new family of warlike kings. In 260 the Persians defeated the Romans and captured the Emperor Valerian.

The problems of running the Empire became too great for one man, and the Empire was split into two. The Emperor Constantine founded a new capital in the East at Constantinople.

But even this was not enough. In 410 Rome itself was sacked. In 476 the last Roman emperor in the West was removed by the tribal chief who commanded his troops. The Roman Empire in the East survived, but became more Greek in language and customs and is often known as the Byzantine Empire (see Sources 39 and 40).

SOURCE 39

Europe at the end of the 5th century. The Roman Empire remains in the East and in the West there are separate tribal kingdoms.

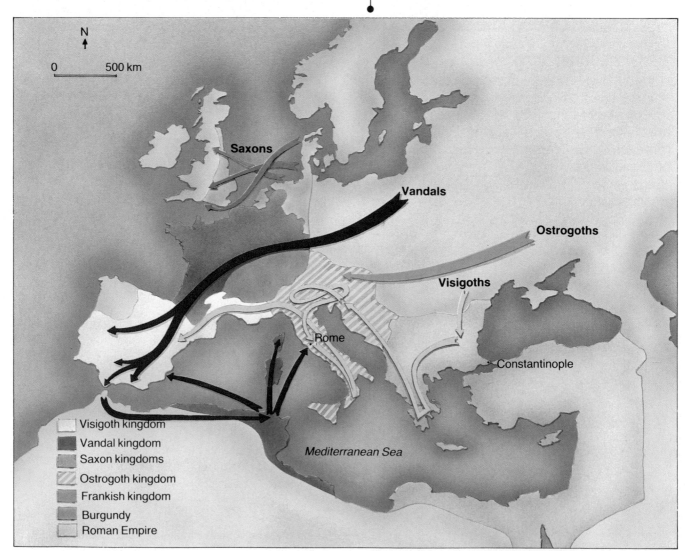

Visigoth kingdom
Vandal kingdom
Saxon kingdoms
Ostrogoth kingdom
Frankish kingdom
Burgundy
Roman Empire

The Emperor Justinian, who ruled from 527 to 565. He was a great conqueror and also organised Roman law. He was the last Eastern Roman emperor to speak Latin.

The end of Roman rule in Britain

Special efforts were made to defend outlying parts of the Empire, such as Britain. Forts like the one in Source 41 were built all along the south and east coasts of Britain to protect the land from Saxon sea raiders. Navies patrolled the seas continuously. These forces were led by the Count of the Saxon Shore.

As things became more difficult for Rome the troops were withdrawn. In 410 the Emperor Honorius wrote to the leaders of Britain telling them that they must look after their own defence.

ACTIVITY

1 Write a letter from a Roman in Britain in AD 410 asking the Emperor Honorius for help against the Saxon invaders.

2 Write a reply from Honorius saying why you cannot send help and offering advice.

3 What will the Roman Britons do on receiving this reply?

SOURCE 41
The Roman 'Saxon Shore' fort at Portchester, Hampshire, built about AD 290. The castle in the top corner is medieval.

The influence of Rome

The influence of the Romans survived for many centuries. This influence can still be found today in many different ways. They include languages, buildings, the Roman Catholic Church and ideas and learning.

Language and buildings

Many of the modern languages of Western Europe are heavily influenced by Latin. These languages are often called Romance languages. Source 42 gives some examples.

Builders have often copied Roman buildings and styles (Source 43), right up to modern times. Roman styles are particularly used for grand public buildings like the one in Source 44.

The Roman Catholic Church

After the removal of the last Western Roman emperor, the Bishop of Rome was the only part of official Roman power left. He became known as the Pope or 'father' (see Source 45). The links between the Church in the West and the emperor in the East slowly broke down. For many centuries the Popes claimed to have overall power in Western Europe, like the emperors had had.

In the West, the Roman Catholic Church kept many Roman ideas alive. Church services were in Latin and the Bible was in Latin. Latin was also used by learned people to communicate. Roman law influenced Church law. Roman books were kept safe in monasteries and new copies made.

SOURCE 42
Some words in Latin and four European languages.

Latin	English	French	Spanish	Italian
populus	people	peuple	pueblo	popolo
sal	salt	sel	sal	sale
turris	turret	tour	torre	torre
leges	laws	lois	leyes	leggei
aqua	water	eau	agua	acqua

SOURCE 43
The courtyard of the Palazzo Farnese, Rome, built in the sixteenth century. The builder copied the style from the nearby Roman ruins of the Theatre of Marcellus and the Colosseum.

SOURCE 44
University College, London, built in the 1820s.

Roman ideas and learning

Many aspects of Roman knowledge disappeared with the end of the Empire: how to make concrete; how to make baked bricks; how to build complex water supply systems. But some knowledge remained. In medicine, for example, the books of Galen, a famous Roman doctor, continued to be used for centuries. Source 46 shows a book of Galen's work, printed in 1565, over 1,350 years after his death.

Roman numbers are not easy to use and they were replaced by the Arabic numbers we use today. But Roman numbers are still found in use (see Source 47).

Latin remained an important part of people's education for many years. Latin is still taught today in many schools, and until the 1970s was taught in many more.

1 The Latin words for 'laws' and 'water' are not very close to the English words. Which English words to do with law and water are closer to the Latin words?

2 Which European language seems to have most in common with Latin?

3 What other buildings do you know in the same style as Source 44?

4 Why do you think this style has been so popular with builders over the centuries?

5 What does the fact that Galen's works were still being published 1,350 years after his death tell us about the progress in medicine in the years in between?

SOURCE 45
Pope Gregory the Great (Pope 590 to 604). In this picture, made much later, he is seen in the centre with arms raised. He is praying for an end to a dreadful plague affecting Rome. Gregory belonged to an old Roman family. He brought Christians in Europe into contact with each other and sent missionaries to Spain and England.

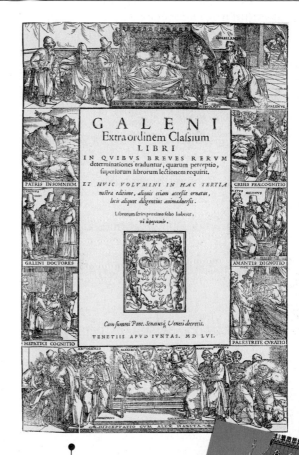

SOURCE 46
Title page of Galen's works, 1565.

SOURCE 47
One use of Roman numbers today.

Glossary

Ancestors
The members of your family who lived before you.

Aqueduct
A channel for water to flow in over a long distance. It might include bridges and tunnels.

Archaeologist
A person who studies the past by looking at the remains, usually by digging for them.

Artillery
Machines for firing missiles, like arrows.

Assassinate
To murder an important politician.

Auxiliary
A soldier of the Roman army who was not a Roman citizen.

Barbarian
To Romans, anyone who lived outside the Empire.

Cavalry
Soldiers who fight on horseback.

Chariot
A small, two-wheeled cart, pulled by horses.

Civil war
War between different groups within the same country.

Dictator
Government by one person on their own.

Dowry
Money or property given by a woman's family to her husband when she marries.

Emperor
A person who rules over an empire.

Empire
Many lands and peoples under one ruler.

Evidence
Information derived from a source about a historical topic.

Infantry
Soldiers who fight on foot.

Inscription
Letters or words carved on a stone or tomb.

Legionary
A Roman soldier who was a Roman citizen.

Life expectancy
The length of time people might be expected to live.

Mosaic
A pattern, or picture, made of small pieces of coloured tile, used to decorate floors and sometimes walls.

Order
A group of people of the same rank, or level, in Roman society. Each order had certain rights and duties.

Peasant
A poor person who lived and worked on the land.

Persecution
Being attacked or treated unfairly because of who you are or what you believe in.

Priest
Someone who carries out religious ceremonies.

Province
A region or part of the empire.

Rampart
A raised wall or earth bank to protect a camp or fort.

Senator
A member of the Senate, and so of the highest order of Roman society.

Sestercius/sesterces
A small coin or coins.

Slave
A person with no rights at all, owned as a piece of property by someone else.

Sling
A weapon for firing stones by whirling them round in a leather loop and then letting go.

Syphon
A means of making water travel uphill in a closed pipe.

Index

Page numbers in **bold** refer to
illustrations/captions

Agricola 11, 54
amphitheatres 22, 23
aqueducts 21, 62
army 4, 6–11
  in action 8–11
  structure and composition 6–7
artillery 6, 11, 62
Augustus 43–4
auxiliaries 4, 7, 62

barbarians 45, 53, 62
basilica 18
baths 20, **21**, **54**
boats and ships 40, 46, 49
Boudicca 52, 53
Britain 4–13, 48
  Christianity 57
  conquest 10–11, 52, 54
  farming 55
  invasion 4–5, 48
  roads **50**, **51**
  towns 54
building 60

Caesar, Julius **5**, **13**, 42–3, 52, 53
Caratacus 10, 52
Carthaginians, wars with 12
Catholicism, Roman 60
cavalry 7, 62
Celts 4, 10, 11, 52, 53, 54, **56**
chariots 5, 62
children 30, 32–3
Christianity 47, 56–7, 60, **61**
cities and towns 14 25
civil war 43, 62
Claudius **43**, 48
clothing 28
Cogidumnus 52, **53**, 54
cooking **19**, 26–7
countryside, farming 25, 55
Cunobelin 52

dictators 42, 62
Domitian 50
dress 28

education 61
emperors 42–5, 62
Empire, Roman
  Christian 57
  decline 58
  growth 11
  Rome and the 46–61
  ruling/governing 36–45
  winning 4–13

entertainment 22–3, 44
Etruscans 11

family 29–33, 44
  law and the 29
farming 25, 55
food **19**, 26–7, 44, 49
forum 18, **36**

Gaius (Caligula) 45
Geta, Hosidius 10
gladiators 23
gods and goddesses
  Celtic **56**
  Roman 24
government/rule 36–45
  in Britain, end 59

Hadrian **13**, 45
Hadrian's wall **13**, 45, **56**
hair and hairstyles 28
Hannibal 11
hill-forts 5, 11
homes 34–5
  family life in the 26–33
  slaves in 30, 41
Honorius 59
houses 34–5

ideas, Roman 61

javelin 6
Julius Caesar **5**, **13**, 42–3, 52, 53
Justinian **59**

kitchens 26
knights 39

language 60
Latin 60, 61
lavatories, public 21
law, families and the 29
learning, Roman 61
legionaries 4, 6, 7, 8, 62
liberti 40

marching-camps 9
marriage 29, 31, 33
medicine 61
Medway, River, crossing of 10
men 29
Mons Graupius, battle of 11

Nero 56
numbers, Roman 61

orders 38, 53, 62

paterfamilias 29, 33, 35
Plautius, Aulus 10
plebs 40
Pompeii 14–15, **16**, **18**, **19**, **20**, **22**, 25, **34**
poor families 32, 33
Pope 60, **61**
priests 24, 62
provinces 11

ramparts 5, 62
religion
  Christian 47, 56–7, 60, **61**
  pre-Christian 24
rich families 30, 33
roads 50–1
Roman Catholicism 60
Rome 46–61
  early 12
  the Empire and 46–61
  influence 60–1
  sacking 58
Romulus and Remus 11
rule **see** government

sacrifices 24
Saxons 59
senators 39, 42, 62
shops 19, **40**
slaves 30, 40, 41, 62
sling(s) 7, 11, 62
society
  divisions (=orders) in 38–41, 53, 62
  families and 29
soldiers 6
sport 22–3
strigil 20, **21**

theatres 22
toga 28
toilets, public 21
towns 14–25
  in Britain 54
trade 46, 49, 52
transport 46, 49, 50–1
travel 46, 51
tribes, Celtic 5

Verica 52
Vesuvius, Mount **14**, 15

wars
  with Carthage 12
  civil 43, 62
water supplies 21
women 29, 30–2

First published 1991 by CollinsEducational
77–85 Fulham Palace Road
Hammersmith
London W6 8JB

ISBN 0 00 327229 – X

Cover design by Glynis Edwards
Book designed by Derek Lee
Series planning by Nicole Lagneau
Edited by Lorimer Poultney
Picture research by Donna Thynne
Artwork by Peter Dennis and Angela Lumley
Production by Mandy Inness

Typeset by Dorchester Typesetting Group Ltd

Printed and bound by Stige Arti Grafiche, Italy

Acknowledgements

Every effort has been made to contact holders of copyright material but if any have been overlooked the publishers will be pleased to make the necessary arrangements at the earliest opportunity.

Photographs The publishers would like to thank the following for permission to reproduce photographs on these pages:

T = top, C = centre, B = bottom, R = right, L = left

Aerofilms, 5B, 59B; Ancient Art & Architecture Collection, 4R, 13, 14L, 19BR, 23B, 24TR, 25C, 28 (hairstyles TR), 39T, 48C; Arbeia Roman Fort, South Shields (Tyne & Wear Museum Service), 53R; Barnaby's Picture Library, London, 43C, 51; D. Sellman/Bath City Council, 54R; Bibliothèque Nationale, 45T; Reproduced by Courtesy of the Trustees of the British Museum, 6, 21T, 30T&BR, 43T, 52CL&CR, 54CL&BL, 57C/Dorchester County Museum, 57B; Cambridge University, Collection of Air Photographs, 9, 17TL, 50; Camera Press Ltd, London, 15, 61BR; Peter Clayton, 19BL, 47, 56; Colchester and Essex Museum, 7R, 43B; Douglas Dickins Photo Library, 21C; C. M. Dixon, 8, 10; E. T. Archive, 61CL; Fishbourne Roman Palace, Sussex Archaeology Trust, 52B, 53L; Werner Forman Archive, 16, 17CR, 19T, 20, 28BL/John Paul Getty Museum, Malibu, 28 (hairstyles BR), 35T, 35B, 36L; Gloucester City Museum and Art Gallery; 7L; C. Haines/Ermine Street Guard, 11L; Sonia Halliday Photographs, 3, 59T; Michael Holford, 14R, 18T, 27B, 32L; Robert Abermann/The Hutchison Picture Library, 27T; Alan Wilkinson/The Hutchinson Picture Library, 27T; Jewry Wall Museum, Leicester, 55; The Mansell Collection Ltd, 12, 17CL, 19CL, 22T&B, 24B, 28T, 28 (hairstyles C), 33T, 34T&B, 40, 42, 44T, 45B, 46T, 48B; Michael Mastronardi, Naples, 39C&B; Museum of London, 26; National Museum of Wales/Ermine Street Guard, 4L; Österreichische Nationalbibliothek, Vienna, 46B; Popperfoto, 24TL; John Ross, 29; Scala, 23T, 30BL, 36–7, 60L; Society of Antiquaries of London, 11R; Rex Features, 18BL; University College London, 60R; Christopher Warde-Jones, Rome, 24C, 25T; The Wellcome Institute, London, 61; Welsh Department of the Environment, 18BR; Roger Wood, 44B; Yorkshire Museum, 31, 32R.

Cover photograph: Sonia Halliday Photographs

The author and publishers gratefully acknowledge permission from the following to reproduce previously published material:

Cambridge University Press for an extract from M. I. Finlay, *The Ancient Economy*, 1973; Oxford University Press for an extract from P. Salway, *Roman Britain*, 1981; Routledge for extracts from J. Wacher, *The Coming of Rome* and S. Frere, *Britannia*.